American Government

President

by Connor Stratton

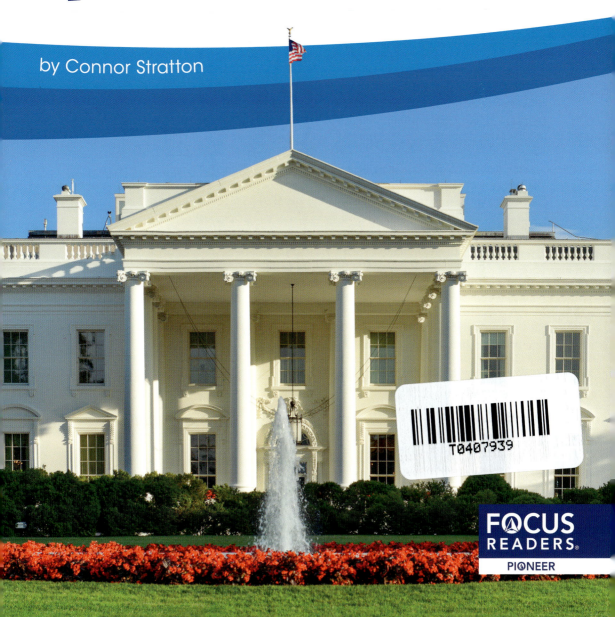

FOCUS READERS®
PIONEER

www.focusreaders.com

Copyright © 2024 by Focus Readers®, Lake Elmo, MN 55042. All rights reserved. No part of this book may be reproduced or utilized in any form or by any means without written permission from the publisher.

Focus Readers is distributed by North Star Editions:
sales@northstareditions.com | 888-417-0195

Produced for Focus Readers by Red Line Editorial.

Photographs ©: Shutterstock Images, cover, 1, 8, 12, 15, 21; Adam Schultz/White House, 4, 11; Spc. Eric Martinez/Multi-National Corps Iraq Public Affairs/DVIDS, 7; Red Line Editorial, 17; Andrea Hanks/White House, 18

Library of Congress Cataloging-in-Publication Data
Names: Stratton, Connor, author.
Title: President / by Connor Stratton.
Description: Lake Elmo, MN : Focus Readers, [2024] | Series: American government | Includes bibliographical references and index. | Audience: Grades 2-3
Identifiers: LCCN 2023002956 (print) | LCCN 2023002957 (ebook) | ISBN 9781637395929 (hardcover) | ISBN 9781637396490 (paperback) | ISBN 9781637397626 (ebook pdf) | ISBN 9781637397060 (hosted ebook)
Subjects: LCSH: Presidents--United States--Juvenile literature.
Classification: LCC JK517 .S77 2024 (print) | LCC JK517 (ebook) | DDC 352.23/70973--dc23/eng/20230213
LC record available at https://lccn.loc.gov/2023002956
LC ebook record available at https://lccn.loc.gov/2023002957

Printed in the United States of America
Mankato, MN
082023

About the Author

Connor Stratton writes and edits nonfiction children's books. He lives in Minnesota.

Table of Contents

CHAPTER 1
The US President 5

CHAPTER 2
Vice President and Cabinet 9

CHAPTER 3
Becoming President 13

 **A CLOSER LOOK**
The Electoral College 16

CHAPTER 4
The Other Branches 19

Focus on the President • 22
Glossary • 23
To Learn More • 24
Index • 24

Chapter 1

The US President

The president leads the United States. She or he is the head of the **government**. She or he runs one branch. This part is called the executive branch. It makes sure **laws** are followed.

Presidents do other jobs, too. They lead the **military**. They also go to other countries. They meet with other leaders. The leaders talk. They come to agreements.

Did You Know? There have been many US presidents. George Washington was the first. He served from 1789 to 1797.

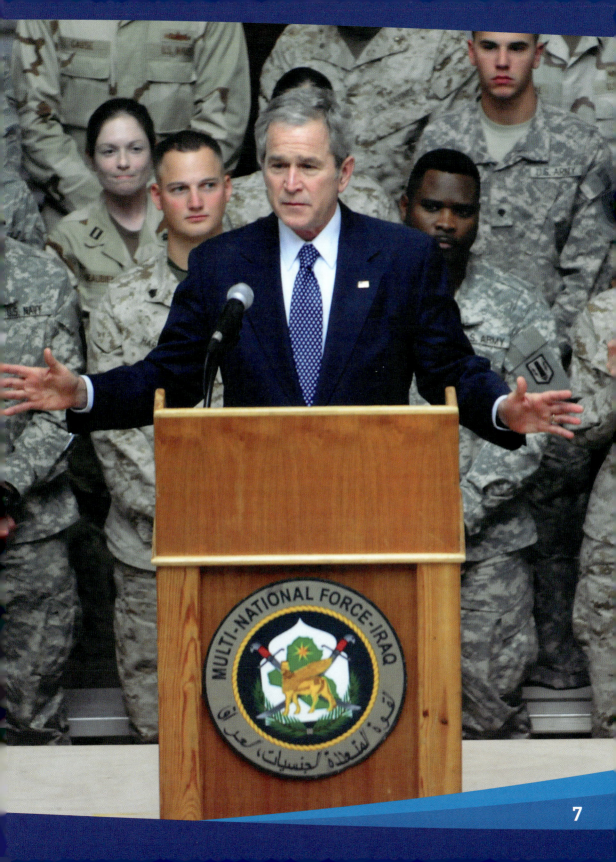

Chapter 2

Vice President and Cabinet

Several people help the president. One person is the vice president. They work as a team. The vice president also takes over if the president dies. He or she becomes the new president.

The cabinet helps, too. This group includes several people. Each has a different job. One person deals with farming. Another deals with schools. One meets with other countries. And some help with money.

Did You Know? Millions of people work for the cabinet members.

Chapter 3

Becoming President

Not everyone can be president. People must be at least 35 years old. They must be born in the United States. They must have lived there for 14 years.

People help pick the president. They vote in an **election**. The winner becomes president. She or he serves for four years. Then another election happens. She or he can **run** one more time.

Did You Know? The president lives in the White House. This building is in Washington, DC.

A Closer Look

The Electoral College

People in each state vote for the president. One person gets the most votes. That person wins the state's **electors**. Some states have more people. They get more electors. One person wins the most electors. He or she becomes president. This system has a name. It is the Electoral College.

Electors by State

*Accurate for 2024 and 2028 presidential elections.

†Washington, DC, is not a state. But it still gets three electors.

Chapter 4

The Other Branches

The president works with other branches. One is the judicial branch. The Supreme Court leads it. **Justices** fill the court. The president helps pick them.

The other branch is the legislative branch. It is led by Congress. It writes **bills**. The president can sign the bills. Then they become laws.

Did You Know? A president can **veto** bills. She or he does not sign them. They usually do not become laws.

FOCUS ON
The President

Write your answers on a separate piece of paper.

1. Write a few sentences describing some of the jobs the US president does.

2. Would you want to meet the president? Why or why not?

3. How old must people be to become president?
    - A. 18 years old
    - B. 35 years old
    - C. 65 years old

4. What might presidents do when they do not want bills to become laws?
    - A. They might vote on the bills.
    - B. They might sign the bills.
    - C. They might veto the bills.

Answer key on page 24.

Glossary

bills
Written plans to make laws.

election
When people vote for who they want in a government job.

electors
People who are part of the Electoral College. They select the president based on votes in each state.

government
The people and groups that run a city, state, tribe, or country.

justices
People who decide cases in courts of law.

laws
Rules made by governments.

military
Soldiers or armed forces.

run
To take part in an election and try to get a job in government.

veto
To not sign a bill from Congress.

To Learn More

BOOKS

Krasner, Barbara. *Exploring the Executive Branch*. Minneapolis: Lerner Publications, 2020.

Walton, Kathryn. *The White House: Home of the First Family*. New York: PowerKids Press, 2023.

NOTE TO EDUCATORS

Visit **www.focusreaders.com** to find lesson plans, activities, links, and other resources related to this title.

Index

C
cabinet, 10

E
Electoral College, 16–17

V
vice president, 9

W
Washington, George, 6

Answer Key: 1. Answers will vary; 2. Answers will vary; 3. B; 4. C

American Government

Governments help our society run smoothly. This series introduces early readers to the different types of government in the United States, exploring their parts, roles, and how people fill their offices.

BOOKS IN THIS SET

Congress

State Governments

Local Governments

Supreme Court

President

Tribal Governments

Focus Readers deliver captivating topics, accessible text, and vibrant visuals to build reading confidence and motivate young readers.

NOTE TO EDUCATORS
Visit www.focusreaders.com to find:
- Lesson plans
- Activities
- Links
- Other resources related to this title

PIONEER
RL: 1–2. IL: 1–3.

ISBN: 978-1-63739-649-0

American Government

Tribal Governments

by Connor Stratton